Domestic Abuse
in Church Communities
 a safe pastoral response

Dedication

For Mimi

Domestic Abuse
in Church Communities
a safe pastoral response

Nikki Dhillon Keane

redemptorist
p u b l i c a t i o n s

Published by Redemptorist Publications
Wolf's Lane, Chawton, Hampshire, GU34 3HQ, UK
Tel: +44 (0)1420 88222, Fax: +44 (0)1420 88805
Email: rp@rpbooks.co.uk, www.rpbooks.co.uk

A registered charity limited by guarantee
Registered in England 3261721

Series Editor: Sr Janet Fearns
Edited by Kathy Dyke
Designed by Eliana Thompson

ISBN 978-0-85231-543-9

A CIP catalogue record for this book is available from the British Library.

The publisher gratefully acknowledges permission to use the following copyright material:

Excerpts from the *New Revised Standard Version Bible: Anglicized Edition*, copyright © 1989,
1995, Division of Christian Education of the National Council of the Churches of Christ in
the United States of America. Used by permission. All rights reserved.

The Power and Control Wheel image (page 12) is included by kind permission of the
Domestic Abuse Intervention Program (DAIP) of Duluth, MN, www.theduluthmodel.org

Every effort has been made to trace copyright holders and to obtain their permission for the
use of copyright material. The publisher apologises for any errors or omissions and would
be grateful for notification of any corrections that should be incorporated in future reprints
or editions of this book.

Printed by Lithgo Press Ltd.,
Leicester, LE8 6NU

Acknowledgements

There are far too many people to name individually, but I would like to
express my deep gratitude to the survivors of domestic abuse who have
contributed their stories, prayers and experiences to help make this book
what it is. Their courage and generosity have been overwhelming.

I would also like to thank the people who have shared their professional
expertise, thoughts and suggestions. Their help has been invaluable.

Lastly, I am, as always, grateful to my husband and daughter for their
long suffering patience, their love and their support.

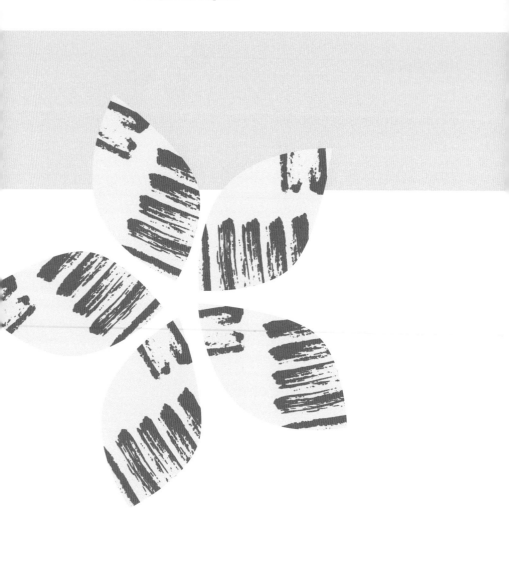

Introduction

Domestic abuse is extremely common. Whether or not you are aware of it, you definitely know someone who has been affected. In any average-sized parish community, it is almost certainly happening in a few families at any one time.

Yet domestic abuse is very rarely mentioned. In recent years new legislation and portrayals of abuse in media drama have given it more attention. This can only be good as it raises awareness and recognition. Support organisations experience increased calls after programmes are aired from people seeking help because they have recognised their own situations reflected in TV or radio dramas. Raising awareness about domestic abuse can undoubtedly save lives.

In the course of my work, I often meet people who would like to offer help and support to those who are dealing with domestic abuse, but are unsure how to proceed. This book aims to help develop your understanding of what domestic abuse is, what difficulties and dangers are faced by those dealing with abuse and what steps you can take to offer safe support. It is written from the perspective of Christian communities, but many of the issues are the same for all religions and cultures. I hope that people from all faith backgrounds or none will also find some useful insights here.

I started working with victims and survivors of domestic abuse around seventeen years ago. Most of my early experience came from my work with people in the Deaf community, where rates of domestic abuse are roughly twice those outside it; one in two Deaf women will experience domestic abuse at some point in their life.[1]

Since then, I have worked with a wide range of victims and survivors and led training events for therapists and people working in church settings to help deepen their understanding of domestic abuse. In 2013 I was invited to join the Catholic Bishops' Conference of England and Wales Domestic Abuse Working Group. The group was set up in response to a domestic homicide review after a husband murdered his Catholic wife and her teenage son who was trying to protect her.

Tragically, it was after another domestic homicide review following the murder of a young Catholic woman by her boyfriend that I was asked to set up a project in Westminster Diocese which became Safe in Faith.

Much of my work is motivated by the fervent wish that victims and survivors who turn to their church community for help will find safe, knowledgeable and robust support and that it won't take yet another domestic homicide review to make it happen.

Research by the American organisation Faith Trust Institute found that victims of domestic abuse with a religious faith are much more likely to turn to their minister of religion than to statutory services.[2] The response they receive can mean the difference between life and death.

Tragedies remind us that domestic abuse can be fatal. If we take a wrong step in our attempts to help it could have disastrous consequences. I hope that this book can guide those wishing to take safe action to end suffering and to save lives.

This book includes stories from survivors. Names and details have been changed to preserve anonymity.

Before we begin, a word of caution: domestic abuse is frighteningly common. Some of you reading this book might have direct experience of being a victim/survivor. Some others may have loved ones who have suffered or even died at the hands of an abusive partner. Because of the nature of this issue, the material in this book may at times be challenging to read. I make no apology for that: it would do a great disservice to victims and survivors everywhere if I presented you with anything less than a truthful and complete account of what domestic abuse is like. However, if you are likely to find some of the content difficult, I would urge you to take good care of yourself: take breaks from reading; do things which strengthen and replenish you; find someone to talk to if you need to. You will find lists of organisations providing support and further information at the end of the book.

Lastly, I would like to thank you for joining the fight to end the suffering of abuse by choosing to read this book. There is a long way to go, but together we can do much.

Seema's story

"My husband never laid a finger on me, but he made my life hell for twenty years. I went to see a counsellor because I was having panic attacks and she helped me see that it was because of the domestic abuse. I didn't believe her at first, but then I found out more about domestic abuse. It was amazing: I just kept thinking 'That's me! That's me!' If I had only known years ago I could have had the help I needed instead of thinking it was just me going crazy."

Endnotes

1 Deaf Hope (www.signhealth.org.uk/deafhope)
2 Faith Trust Institute (www.faithtrustinstitute.org)

1

What is domestic abuse?

There are many different beliefs about domestic abuse, unfortunately often based on inaccurate or misleading ideas. I have seen people attempt to offer support without appreciating the challenges or level of danger involved: they have actually done more harm than good.

Domestic abuse is potentially fatal. Any attempt at support, particularly from a reconciliation-focused approach, has the potential to put lives at risk. All the guidance in this book is based on a safety-focused approach. The safety of all concerned, including helpers, is paramount, but in particular the safety of those at most risk: victim/survivors and children.

The first four chapters of this book aim to develop understanding of domestic abuse, what it is and how it affects people. This knowledge is essential before any kind of support can be given. Later chapters will explore some ways to offer safe and meaningful support to people who are being or have been abused.

Terminology

There have been recent attempts to update abuse-related language. Because these words and phrases describe powerfully emotional things, people can have strong reactions to them. It can be helpful to understand why some terms are generally preferred over others, but above all, it's important to respect the choices of people who are dealing with these issues in their lives. Below, I have explained the terms I have chosen to use in this book, but when I am working with individuals, I tend to follow the language that they choose to use.

Domestic violence

This is a more traditional term, although it is still used by many organisations (for example the National Domestic Violence Helpline). This term tends to suggest that only physical violence counts as domestic abuse. Dangerous abuse can be unrecognised because physical violence has not been present.

Intimate partner violence (IPV)

IPV has come into use more recently. It can be useful because the word "domestic" gives the impression that a victim and perpetrator must live together, which isn't always the case (particularly with the growing issue of dating abuse amongst teenagers). However, it is only useful when the perpetrator is a spouse or partner, which is not always the case.

Domestic abuse/ Domestic violence and abuse (DVA)

Domestic abuse or DVA are more inclusive terms because they recognise all the different forms of domestic abuse. They also recognise that any family member can be a perpetrator of domestic abuse. They are the terms I am most likely to use.

Victim/survivor

Some people working in this field don't like to use the term "victim" because it seems to be disempowering. However, in my experience, many individuals find it helpful to explore their journey and to identify what it means to them to move from victim to survivor. These are powerful words, and when I am dealing with individuals I always give them the space to choose for themselves which label has the most meaning. When I am talking or writing about abuse in general, I tend to use the term "victim/survivor" unless I am referring specifically to one or the other.

Perpetrator

This is the term generally used to refer to the person carrying out the abuse, although "abuser" is also sometimes used. Some people are uncomfortable with the word "perpetrator" because it can bring up powerful emotions, particularly because of its association with child abuse. While it can sometimes be tempting to use more comfortable language, it is important to recognise that we are dealing with a serious and often life-threatening issue, and that when language is uncomfortable it is because the subject itself is challenging.

In situations of domestic abuse, there is always someone who is a perpetrator and someone who is a victim/survivor. These are not interchangeable roles. Perpetrators and victim/survivors don't always behave in ways we might expect, but the nature of abuse is that the perpetrator is always the perpetrator and the victim/ survivor is always the victim/survivor, whether or not it is evident to an onlooker at any given moment.

Defining domestic abuse

In 2013 the UK government defined domestic abuse as:

> any incident or pattern of incidents of controlling, coercive, threatening behaviour, violence or abuse between those aged sixteen or over who are, or have been, intimate partners or family members, regardless of gender or sexuality.[1]

Domestic abuse can occur in any kind of family relationship, not just romantic partners or spouses. It includes a range of abusive behaviours, not just physical violence. However, when thinking about domestic abuse, most people will describe physical violence with visible injuries. I have met professionals who didn't identify a situation of abuse because the abuse wasn't physical. The victims were consequently left to suffer and didn't get the support they needed. Even more frequently, I meet victims of abuse who know that something is wrong, but don't realise that what they are experiencing is domestic abuse, because their experience doesn't match their narrow understanding of abuse. Consequently, they don't seek out the right kind of help and often continue suffering.

Domestic abuse and the law

Domestic abuse falls within two different kinds of law:

1. Criminal law punishes offenders who commit a crime through the CPS (Crown Prosecution Service). Domestic abuse is not in itself a crime in most of the UK, but several behaviours associated with abuse are criminal (for example rape or assault). Since December 2015, coercive control is also a criminal offence.

2. Civil law protects victim/survivors through the family or county courts. They generally deal with things like most kinds of injunctions (other than restraining orders) and child contact after divorce.

Despite moves to improve domestic abuse-related criminal and civil law, many victim/survivors still feel that they are not sufficiently protected.[2]

The different kinds of domestic abuse

Below is a list of the main kinds of domestic abuse. In most cases, more than one form is present.

Psychological

This can include threats, gas-lighting (making someone doubt their own reality), mind games and mental torture. It is listed first because it almost always the foundation of all other kinds of abuse. Elements of psychological abuse can be used to groom victims for other kinds of abuse, although by itself it can cause devastating and lasting damage to the victim. Psychological abuse is a way of wearing down the victim to make them easier to control, giving the perpetrator power over them.

Emotional

Emotional abuse uses constant criticism, put-downs, emotional withdrawal or belittling the effects of abuse. It includes any action which hurts the victim emotionally, damages self-esteem, causes them to feel weaker and empowers the perpetrator to maintain control.

Isolation

This powerfully effective form of psychological abuse deserves special attention. It is much harder to control someone who is surrounded by loving and supportive people. Perpetrators might:

- insist on moving to a different area, far from the victim's friends and family;
- gradually undermine the victim's relationships;
- sow seeds of doubt and mistrust, until relationships are damaged, sometimes beyond repair;
- (often used later) become so aggressive when the victim does try to see friends or family that it becomes easier just to stop.

Isolation:

- makes a victim easier to control;
- deprives a victim of crucial social contact;
- can profoundly damage psychological and physical health.

Physical

This refers to any kind of physical violence: not just hitting or kicking but also burning, choking, biting, shaking, shoving and physically restraining someone. Threats of physical violence (for example holding someone at the top of the stairs and threatening to throw them down) are also physical abuse.

Perpetrators:

- often carefully cause injuries only where they will not be visible to others;

- do not abuse because of losing control of their temper;

- use physical abuse to gain and maintain control of their victim.

Sexual

Sexual abuse refers to a range of abusive acts which include not only rape, but any non-consensual sexual activity. Several abusive behaviours might not be recognised as sexual abuse. These include:

- forcing the victim/survivor to agree to have sex in order to avoid other kinds of abusive behaviour;

- sexual name-calling or shaming;

- force or pressure:

  - to watch porn;

  - to take part in or watch sexual acts with another person;

  - to wear highly sexualised clothing;

  - to cover up their bodies in public against their wishes and regardless of additional cultural pressures to dress in a certain way;

- any behaviour which uses sex or sexual activity in order to gain power and control over another person.

Sexual abuse is probably much more common that most people realise, because not only do most cases go unreported, many victims don't recognise it as abuse.

Economic

Economic abuse can take different forms. The perpetrator might:

- prevent or discourage their victim from working;
- force their partner to earn money so that they don't have to work themselves;
- control all the money;
- expect the victim to account for every penny they spend;
- force the victim to take out a loan or withhold money so that they cannot buy essentials like food for the children;
- use money to gain power and control over the victim.

Economic abuse disproportionately affects women.[3]

Neglect

When we talk about neglect, most people think about child abuse, but adults can also be victims of neglect. One adult may depend on another individual because:

- they are elderly or frail;
- they have a learning disability, a physical disability or an illness;
- they have a mental health problem;
- they don't speak the local language.

When someone intentionally fails to meet the needs of an individual who relies on them, that is neglect and it is a form of domestic abuse.

Stalking, harassment and digital abuse

This is a common form of abuse after someone has ended a relationship. With the availability of social media, digital abuse has become an increasing problem. Stalking and harassment can be signs that a perpetrator could be extremely dangerous, even if they have not yet been physically violent.

Spiritual

Spiritual abuse is a form of domestic abuse which is still largely unrecognised. Chapter 4 explores spiritual abuse and how it is used by perpetrators to control their victims.

Power and control

Power and control are the central focus of any abusive relationship. In the 1980s, in the USA, a group of survivors created a diagram which has become known as the Duluth Power and Control Wheel (see page 12). This enabled survivors, rather than professionals, to describe their experience.

The Duluth model[4] has become a well-recognised tool for understanding abuse. They have since developed a series of wheels to describe different aspects of abusive relationships. Those of you who are familiar with the excellent book *Living with the Dominator*[5] may recognise that the characters of different "dominators" are based on the Duluth model. This model can help us to understand what motivates perpetrators and how abusive relationships develop.

Endnotes

1 www.gov.uk/guidance/domestic-violence-and-abuse
2 To find out more about domestic abuse and the law, visit www.gov.uk/guidance/domestic-violence-and-abuse
3 Nicola Sharp-Jeffs,"Money Matters: research into the extent and nature of financial abuse within intimate relationships in the UK": https://www.refuge.org.uk/files/Money-Matters.pdf
4 www.theduluthmodel.org
5 Pat Craven, *Living with the Dominator* (London: Freedom Publishing, 2008), also available as a free download

POWER AND CONTROL

USING COERCION AND THREATS
Making and/or carrying out threats to do something to hurt her • threatening to leave her, to commit suicide, to report her to welfare • making her drop charges • making her do illegal things.

USING INTIMIDATION
Making her afraid by using looks, actions, gestures • smashing things • destroying her property • abusing pets • displaying weapons.

USING EMOTIONAL ABUSE
Putting her down • making her feel bad about herself • calling her names • making her think she's crazy • playing mind games • humiliating her • making her feel guilty.

USING ECONOMIC ABUSE
Preventing her from getting or keeping a job • making her ask for money • giving her an allowance • taking her money • not letting her know about or have access to family income.

USING ISOLATION
Controlling what she does, who she sees and talks to, what she reads, where she goes • limiting her outside involvement • using jealousy to justify actions.

USING MALE PRIVILEGE
Treating her like a servant • making all the big decisions • acting like the "master of the castle" • being the one to define men's and women's roles

USING CHILDREN
Making her feel guilty about the children • using the children to relay messages • using visitation to harass her • threatening to take the children away.

MINIMIZING, DENYING AND BLAMING
Making light of the abuse and not taking her concerns about it seriously • saying the abuse didn't happen • shifting responsibility for abusive behavior • saying she caused it.

PHYSICAL VIOLENCE SEXUAL

DOMESTIC ABUSE INTERVENTION PROGRAMS
202 East Superior Street, Duluth, Minnesota 55802
218-722-2781, www.theduluthmodel.org

Mary's story: Living in a coffin

"It was built slowly – it felt cosy at first, safe to be held, affirming to have someone so interested in me. He had good qualities – he was kind, good with other people's children. I knew he had problems: a difficult relationship with his mother, siblings and people at work, but I could help. And I did.

Things weren't perfect, but wasn't that just life? Dad said 'I'm worried about you.' But there were good times and I knew life was never easy.

Odd things happened. Others noticed. 'I won't call you when he's there – I don't want to upset him.' I would invite people round at the weekend: he's more cheerful with people around. 'He's depressed,' I thought 'He left his job to look after the children – I need to be a supportive wife.'

Things worsened. We sought help. The counsellor listened to him shout at me as I sat shaking with tears running down my cheeks. I felt defenceless and scared – I must be supportive, marriage is for life. The coffin kept me in the dark, but the pain of living in it grew.

Concern from my family. Slowly feeling that maybe things were too wrong, maybe this isn't what God intended.

A retreat for marriages in crisis. Months of trying, trying, trying. Making progress, slipping back. Prayers, alone and sometimes together.

Shouting in the car, the children mostly learning to stay quiet. Sometimes the youngest would challenge him. I was afraid for them if they spoke up for me.

A crack in the coffin, a ray of light. The retreat leader said, 'This is not a marriage as God intended. This is an abusive relationship.' 'Really?' I asked. 'God doesn't ask you to stay in this. The Church doesn't ask you to stay in this.' I pondered it in my heart.

Perhaps he could not change, perhaps it was too difficult. More light into the coffin. Where was God in all this? The slow understanding that God does not ask us to stay in unsafe places. Another crack, another ray of light.

Slow, slow awakening. The long decision to leave. Heart pounding as I gathered documents and copied photographs when he was out of the house. Leaving caused trouble. I knew it would.

But healing came, slowly. 'I thought we had lost you,' my sister said. 'I'm so glad you're back.'

Slowly healing. Finding my voice again. Seeing the children healing.

Counselling with someone who understood abusive relationships. Learning to recognise when the voice inside was internalised abuse. I can do it, I thought, with God's help. I can be transformed.

Building a new life, finding my old self, learning to forgive and heal. The coffin is broken, and is slowly being used as firewood. The years not lost. The healing continues."

2

Who is affected by domestic abuse?

Domestic abuse is frighteningly common. These are some of the more shocking statistics.

In the UK:

- One in four women will experience domestic abuse at some point in their life.[1]
- Twenty-five per cent of all reported rapes are connected to domestic abuse.[2]
- Every six seconds a woman is assaulted in her home.[3]
- Every week an average of two women are murdered by their partner or ex-partner.[4]
- Every week up to ten women commit suicide as a result of domestic abuse.[5]

This last statistic (from the organisation Advocacy after Fatal Domestic Abuse) is not very well known, but is extremely important because it shows us very clearly that not just physical abuse, but psychological abuse can also be fatal.

Domestic abuse:

- can affect men and women of any age group;
- happens across every culture and socio-economic group and across every level of education;
- is often unrecognised because people don't fit the expected socio-economic profile.

Women between the ages of sixteen and twenty-four and men between the ages of sixteen and nineteen are particularly at risk.[6] It is possible that victims from wealthier socio-economic backgrounds would be more likely to seek support from the private sector, and if this is the case it would mean that they don't show up in official statistics.

Domestic abuse in different groups

While statistics show that domestic abuse affects people from all walks of life, there are some groups of people who may face additional difficulties as a result of domestic abuse.

People living with a chronic illness or disability

People who have a disability:

- are twice as likely to be a victim of domestic abuse in all its forms (not just neglect).[7] Statistics show that fifty per cent of disabled or deaf women will experience domestic abuse at some point in their lifetime.[8] There is also a higher risk of having been a victim of sexual abuse in childhood.[9]

- may have high levels of dependency, thereby leaving the victim completely trapped.

The perpetrator might:

- be the victim's main carer;

- use someone's disability or illness against them by;

  - withholding or threatening to withhold medication;

  - withholding access to aids like wheelchairs or crutches;

  - refusing to help with essential tasks like washing or eating;

  - accompanying their victim to medical appointments, limiting opportunities to report abuse.

People who have difficulty communicating because they have a speech impairment or have hearing difficulties can find it more difficult to report abuse or to access information and support.

People who have a learning disability are particularly vulnerable to abuse, and are less likely to report it. Even when they do, they are less likely to be believed.

Young people

Dating abuse (abuse in relationships between young people who are dating) is increasingly common. In spite of efforts to educate young people about safe relationships, research has shown a shocking level of normalisation of abusive behaviour. With easy access through smartphones and similar devices, large numbers of young people are developing their understanding of sexual relationships through watching pornography. This can lead to confusion around consent issues and normalisation of unhealthy or inappropriate sexual behaviour.

A study in 2009 carried out by Bristol University and the NSPCC also found that twenty-five per cent of young girls and eighteen per cent of young boys had experienced physical violence from their boyfriend or girlfriend and seventy-five per cent of young girls and fifty per cent of young boys had experienced emotional dating abuse.[10] The study also showed up some worrying attitudes – for example, a large number of young girls thought that a girl could invite physical violence if she flirted with another boy.

Some, although not all, normalisation of abusive behaviour comes from young people who have witnessed or experienced domestic abuse in the home, for example when teenage boys model the behaviours of their abusive fathers and can in turn become abusive towards their mothers and other female relatives.

There is a high risk that young people who have witnessed abuse in the home will normalise it, but often the greater danger is that this makes them vulnerable to becoming victims of abuse later in life. Studies have shown that people who suffered or witnessed abuse as children have a significantly higher risk of experiencing domestic abuse as an adult. This is known as intergenerational abuse.

Anyone can become a victim of domestic abuse. There are many victim/survivors who have never previously experienced abuse, but someone with abuse in their history is particularly vulnerable: the behaviour's familiarity makes it more difficult to recognise abuse and to seek help.

Children

Statistics from the NSPCC[11] show that one in five children in the UK have been exposed to domestic abuse. Of these, a third have also experienced another form of abuse. Perpetrators commonly begin by abusing their spouse and then progress to abusing their children. Children exposed to domestic abuse are more likely to have behavioural or emotional difficulties. It is a safeguarding issue when children have witnessed domestic abuse, even if they are not physically harmed by it.

Older people

Elder abuse:

- can happen in any family;

- can take the form of physical abuse and neglect or, very commonly, financial abuse.

The perpetrator can be the main carer, often a spouse, son or daughter, and dementia can cause the victim extreme difficulties:

- in understanding and reporting abuse;

- in being believed.

People who are far from their country of origin

People who are living in a different country from their friends and family:

- are already isolated;

- find it much harder to access support, particularly if they don't speak the local language;

- may be afraid to approach the police or other authorities for help in cases of insecure immigration status;

- may be threatened if the perpetrator uses insecure immigration status as a controlling threat.

They may find linguistically and culturally accessible services provided by some organisations.

Certain kinds of abuse, like female genital mutilation (FGM), are culturally based and are perpetrated specifically on girls. FGM is a cultural, not a religious, practice and victims can have any religious faith.

LGBT+ communities

Domestic abuse can happen in lesbian and gay relationships, and between people who have trans or non-binary gender identities. Statistics show that eighty per cent of transgender people have experienced domestic abuse at some point in their lives.[12] Some domestic abuse can involve homophobic or transphobic abuse. An additional form of abuse for victims who are not "out" is for the perpetrator to threaten to expose the victim's sexual or gender identity to their family or community.

Sometimes it is more difficult for LGBT people to access support, particularly if they are not open about their sexual identity. LGBT people may find it difficult accessing support (Broken Rainbow, the UK organisation offering support for LGBT victims and survivors of domestic abuse, closed in 2016). People may feel unable to turn to their church community for support because they don't know what sort of response they will find. Some victims seeking support find rejection and condemnation because of their sexual or gender identity.

Men

An average of one in six men experience domestic abuse at some point in their life,[13] and perpetrators who commit abuse against them can be male or female. There are also some additional difficulties in accessing support which are faced by male victims:

- There is a social stigma attached to male victims.
- Male victims are often taken less seriously.
- Many support agencies are geared towards female victims only and cannot cater for male victims.

Women

In spite of the numbers of male victims, domestic abuse is often described as a form of gender-based violence.

Women:

- are disproportionately affected by domestic, sexual and financial abuse;

- are less likely to have access to an independent income which would make it easier to leave an abusive relationship.

Women who are victims of extreme violence or who are killed as a result of domestic abuse significantly outnumber male victims.[14] Women who kill their male partner may do so out of self-defence or desperation after years of abuse – this scenario was dramatised in the BBC Radio 4 soap opera *The Archers*.

Since the first women's refuges were opened in the early 1970s, the biggest reduction has been not in the number of women who are murdered, but the number of women who kill their husbands.[15] This is possibly because, before the existence of refuges, many women victims could see no other way out of their situation.

"Power and control are
the central focus of any
abusive relationship."

Endnotes

1 Women's Aid (www.womensaid.org.uk)
2 "Alcohol, Domestic Abuse and Sexual Assault", Institute of Alcohol Studies (www.ias.org.uk)
3 The Freedom Programme (www.freedomprogramme.co.uk)
4 Women's Aid (www.womensaid.org.uk)
5 Advocacy after Fatal Domestic Abuse (https://aafda.org.uk)
6 Smith et al (2011), quoted in NICE guidelines (www.nice.org.uk)
7 Women's Aid (www.womensaid.org.uk)
8 Deaf Hope (signhealth.org.uk/deafhope)
9 "We Have the Right To Be Safe: protecting disabled children from abuse",
   NSPCC (www.nspcc.org.uk)
10 Barter (2009), "Partner Exploitation and Violence in Teenage Intimate Relationships", NSPCC
   (nspcc.org.uk)
11 Radford et al (2011), "Child Abuse and Neglect in the UK Today", quoted in NSPCC facts and
   statistics (nspcc.org.uk)
12 Scottish Transgender Alliance (2010), "Out of Sight, Out of Mind? Transgender people's
   experience of domestic abuse", www.scottishtrans.org, quoted by Stonewall (www.stonewall.
   org.uk)
13 Mankind Initiative (www.mankind.org.uk)
14 Women's Aid (www.womensaid.org.uk/information-support/what-is-domestic-abuse/
   domestic-abuse-is-a-gendered-crime)
15 Li Eriksson and Paul Mazerolle, "A General Strain Theory of Intimate Partner Homicide",
   Aggression and Violent Behavior (2013): https://doi.org/10.1016/j.avb.2013.07.002; Anna Aizer
   and Pedro Dal Bó, "Love, Hate and Murder: Commitment devices in violent relationships",
   J Public Econ (2013)

3

How does domestic abuse happen?

What motivates one human being to abuse another? Why does someone stay in a relationship that causes so much suffering?

There is a common, very damaging and completely mistaken belief that victims choose to stay because at some level they enjoy being abused, or they want to suffer. I have also heard people say that victims stay because they are too weak to leave. The truth is that nobody chooses abuse. Victim/survivors of domestic abuse are among the strongest and bravest people I have met. In the face of so much misinformation, if we wish to be of help, it is important to be clear about how domestic abuse really happens and what the causes are.

- Perpetrators don't behave abusively at the start of a relationship. If they did, then no one would ever get involved with them.

- There is almost always a period of "grooming" where a perpetrator will be charming and attentive; sometimes they will make their victim feel like the luckiest person in the world to have found such a partner.

- Then the psychological and emotional abuse will start, gradually chipping away at the victim's confidence so that they don't feel anyone else would want to be with them. The perpetrator then feels secure enough to display more controlling and abusive behaviour.

- They will start disrupting the victim's relationships with family and friends. Under the guise of "looking after" their victim they might:

  - demand to know where they are at every second, whom they are with, to whom they have spoken;

  - check phone and email messages and social media;

  - display extreme jealousy but explain it as deep love;

- encourage the victim to give up work, or suggest moving far away, increasing isolation and introducing financial abuse.

The more trapped and isolated the victim becomes, the more the perpetrator feels able to show their true colours. The psychological abuse becomes worse and physical and sexual abuse may be introduced.

In most cases, the abuse will happen sporadically, with periods of the old charming behaviour in between (see the cycle of abuse diagram opposite) which makes it harder to understand what is happening. Underneath this is a general pattern of escalation – the more trapped the victim becomes, the worse the abuse becomes.

There is a very common pattern that abuse becomes worse after a couple becomes engaged, worse still after marriage and yet still worse after children are born. Pregnancy is a high-risk time for victims of abuse. A high percentage (around thirty per cent) of victims experience physical abuse for the first time when they are pregnant.[1] There is also a higher risk of more extreme violence and abuse during pregnancy. These attacks can sometimes result in injuries to the unborn baby, or even miscarriage or stillbirth, as well as a higher risk of more dangerous or fatal injuries to the mother.

Many people believe that getting married or having a baby can help to heal the difficulties in a problem relationship. If even low-level abuse or control is already present, these statistics would suggest that getting married or starting a family could significantly increase the risk of abuse becoming more dangerous.

The cycle of abuse

Below is a diagram of the Cycle of Abuse. Almost every abusive relationship will follow this cycle, although the time frames can vary drastically. In some cases, the whole cycle can last a few hours, while for other people it can last months or even years.

The "honeymoon period" creates confusion: it is very easy to believe that the perpetrator has mended their ways and that the nightmare of abuse is over. The perpetrator's behaviour:

- is so different that victims can question whether the abuse was as bad as they remembered, or whether it really happened at all;

- can convince their victim that they imagined the abuse.

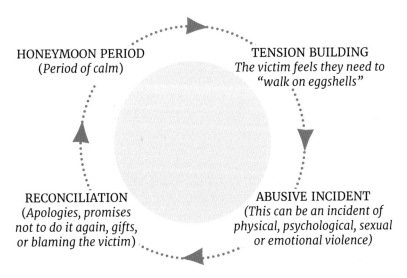

HONEYMOON PERIOD
(*Period of calm*)

TENSION BUILDING
The victim feels they need to "walk on eggshells"

RECONCILIATION
(*Apologies, promises not to do it again, gifts, or blaming the victim*)

ABUSIVE INCIDENT
(*This can be an incident of physical, psychological, sexual or emotional violence*)

So how does someone become trapped in this cycle? If things are that bad, why doesn't the victim just leave?

Many people working in the field of domestic abuse would argue that this is the wrong question. Asking why the victim doesn't leave puts responsibility on the victim for the continuation of the abuse and is actually a form of victim blaming. Instead, experts say, we should be asking why the perpetrator abuses.

25

It is actually just as important to ask the first question. If we wish to really help someone who is experiencing domestic abuse, it is absolutely vital to understand the different things which make it difficult or dangerous to leave. Without a proper understanding of those difficulties, we may suggest inappropriate or dangerous courses of action, or find ourselves becoming frustrated or impatient with people because we don't appreciate their problems. In no way does this suggest that the victim is in any way responsible. On the contrary, it is vital to appreciate exactly how difficult and terrifying it can be to consider leaving an abusive relationship.

Each individual, their situation and the challenges they face are unique, but below is a list of some of the most common reasons why victims of domestic abuse might find it difficult to leave.

Fear of death

Perpetrators may threaten to kill the victim if they try to leave, and these are threats which need to be taken very seriously. The most dangerous time for a victim of domestic abuse is the period just before and just after leaving the relationship. You are seventy times more likely to be killed in the two weeks after leaving than at any other time.[2]

Threats

It is common for perpetrators to make other threats in order to prevent their victim from leaving, for example that they will burn down the house and/or hurt loved ones or pets. Some perpetrators threaten to commit suicide in order to make a victim feel unable to leave.

Nowhere to go

When someone has been isolated from friends and family, there is often nowhere safe for them to go to. Many victims are trapped economically because of financial abuse. It is a common belief that any victim of domestic abuse can easily find a safe place in a refuge, but the reality is sadly very different. On just one day in 2017 94 women and 90 children were turned away from refuges because there was no space for them.[3] (There are, at present in the UK, around 275 women's refuges and approximately 1500 animal refuges.[4]) Most refuges for women will not accept any males over the age of twelve, meaning that any woman with a teenage son would not be able to find a safe space with their child.

In addition to this, as a result of the abuse, many victim/survivors have been isolated from friends, family or anyone else who may be able to offer support. Attempting to reach out to someone, for example in their local community or parish, would involve disclosing the abuse which is often difficult or even dangerous.

Threats to children

Many perpetrators will threaten to harm children or to take children away if their victim tries to leave. If a victim has ever struggled as a parent, had too much alcohol, made a mistake or lost their temper, the perpetrator can use this to threaten to report them to social services as an unfit parent. When a perpetrator has family or connections in another country, there is a very real risk that they might abduct children and take them abroad.

Fears around shared access to children

When children are involved, it is likely that the victim/survivor will need to co-parent with the abuser. This will create ongoing opportunities to carry on the abuse, often through the children. For some victim/survivors they are choosing between two different abusive situations rather than an escape from abuse.

Sense of duty

This is something which is commonly experienced by victim/survivors of abuse. It can be particularly common with people whose religious or cultural beliefs might lead them to feel that they have to forgive and stay with their spouse no matter what, even when their physical or psychological safety, or that of their children, is at risk. Some of the psychological effects of abuse can also lead victim/survivors to feel a sense of responsibility for their abuser, even when that puts them in danger.

Low self-esteem

One of the most powerful ways in which domestic abuse affects a victim/survivor is the destruction of their self-esteem. This has two devastating effects which can keep a person trapped:

- a sense of worthlessness: they don't deserve any better than the abuse;

- a feeling of powerlessness: it seems futile to attempt to change their situation.

Feelings of guilt and shame

It may seem strange to feel guilty or ashamed for things another person has done to you, but these are very common feelings generated by the effects of the abuse itself. Perpetrators are skilled at projecting blame onto their victim. When this happens over an extended period, the victim learns to accept inappropriate feelings of blame for their treatment. These feelings prevent many victims from seeking help.

Belief that the perpetrator will change

Perpetrators are usually very skilled at convincing their victim (and others) of their genuine remorse and desire to mend their ways. As we can see in the cycle of abuse diagram on page 25, the honeymoon period can last a long time and it is easy to believe that the abuse has ended. This common coping strategy helps victims survive as they hope that one day things might be different. It is particularly common when the victim's faith teaches messages of redemption and forgiveness.

Feelings of love for the perpetrator

How could anyone have feelings of love for their abuser?

- This is the same person the victim fell in love with and chose as their partner (although their partner's abusive potential was not apparent at the time).

- During the honeymoon phases, the perpetrator will appear as the same person the victim was first in a relationship with, sometimes for long periods of time.

- The differences between the honeymoon phases and the abuse can be so drastic that victims often say it is like living with two different people.

- It is possible to still feel deep feelings of love for the person's "nice side".

The victim doesn't realise it is abuse

Many people know they are deeply unhappy or even afraid, but don't realise they are in an abusive relationship. This may be because:

- the abuse doesn't match their understanding of what an abusive relationship looks like (perhaps because there is little or no physical abuse);

- the gradual onset has made it difficult to recognise;

- people don't understand about the cycle of abuse. If the perpetrator is sometimes loving and caring, can it really be an abusive relationship?

Sometimes a victim/survivor needs time and support to realise that this is an abusive relationship before they can act to protect themselves.

Exhaustion

It is easy to underestimate the amount of energy needed for a victim to keep themselves and their children alive and relatively safe from one day to the next. When it takes up every ounce of energy, the thought of dealing with all the difficulties described above is more than many people can cope with.

Why does the perpetrator abuse?

Now we come to the second important question: why does someone abuse the very person they are meant to love and cherish?

There are many ideas about how people become perpetrators of abuse, and almost all of them are false. Many are so widely believed that it is worth taking a moment to explain why they are not true. Any of the following things could, in some situations, be factors which might make existing abuse worse, but none of them are actually causes of abuse. The cause is something else entirely.

Myth 1: They do it because they have a mental health problem

It is true that there are some perpetrators who have a mental health problem or personality disorder (for example, there are suggestions that it is not uncommon for some perpetrators to show signs of narcissistic personality disorder, while others might have an anxiety disorder or depression).

These problems might make the abuse worse at times or influence the kind of abuse that is perpetrated, but they are not the underlying cause.

Many people with similar mental health problems never behave in abusive ways. Many perpetrators don't have any kind of mental illness. A mental health problem might affect when and how abuse occurs, but it isn't the reason it happens.

Myth 2: They do it because they have an alcohol or drug problem

It is true that there are links between alcohol or drug use and domestic abuse. But alcohol and drug abuse are not causes of domestic abuse. No amount of alcohol turns a non-abusive person into a perpetrator.

However, if someone is already abusive, alcohol and some other drugs lower their inhibitions and can make the abuse worse, or more violent. Someone who is abusive and struggling with things they find difficult to control is likely to use abusive behaviour in order to feel more powerful again. So an abusive person who is dealing with addiction or withdrawal is likely to become more abusive. That doesn't mean that alcohol or drugs make them abusive, it just complicates and worsens an already abusive situation.

Myth 3: They do it because they have anger issues or problems controlling their temper

This is a very common misconception. However, domestic abuse is not caused by an anger management problem.

A perpetrator will use anger and aggression to control and intimidate their victim. If they really had difficulty controlling themselves, they would lose control and behave aggressively in all sorts of situations, at work, with friends and in their communities. In fact, most perpetrators are very charming with other people: they are only abusive with their victim.

It is easy to misinterpret an abusive incident as a loss of control. Some victims report that while they are being attacked their abuser's face looks wild and out of control. Yet the abuser is still able to exert enough self-control to ensure they only hit their victim in places where it won't show.

Myth 4: They do it because of their culture or religion

This is probably the "cause" of domestic abuse I hear most often. However, evidence shows that abuse happens across cultures, socio-economic groups and religions. Perpetrators from every faith or culture can and do use twisted versions of cultural traditions or faith teachings in order to subjugate their victims. Sometimes culture might affect the way abuse might manifest itself, but abuse itself is present everywhere.

It may be a little comforting to think that it is less likely to happen among groups of people who are similar to you, but in fact domestic abuse is happening all around us. It could be happening to your neighbour, or the person sitting next to you in church. Someone you know and admire could be a perpetrator, and someone you would never guess is suffering could be a victim or survivor.

Myth 5: They do it because they were a victim of abuse in the past

This is a particularly damaging myth. Many survivors of childhood abuse, in addition to all the pain they are dealing with, fear that they will one day harm their own children. **The vast majority of victims and survivors of abuse do not go on to abuse anyone.**

Some perpetrators of abuse have experienced or witnessed abuse in the past and have normalised that behaviour. However, there are also perpetrators who have no history of childhood abuse. Survivors of childhood abuse are more likely to become victims than perpetrators of domestic abuse in adulthood.

So if abuse isn't caused by any of the reasons above, why does it happen?

Experts working with perpetrators have found that there is one thing which all abusers seem to have: a sense of entitlement. Perpetrators of abuse apparently share in common:

- a belief that they are completely entitled to behave in that way towards their victim;

- a sense of superiority and ownership in their attitudes towards the victim;

- a need for power and control in order to feel better about themselves, particularly when they might be feeling powerless in other ways.

Feelings of insecurity or vulnerability are risk factors for abusive behaviour to worsen, and the perpetrator becomes much very much more dangerous if they feel that:

- their abuse has been exposed;

- they are losing control over their victim (for example if the victim wants to leave the relationship).

This finding fits with the Duluth model we looked at earlier, which sees power and control as the central focus of all the different forms of domestic abuse.

Domestic abuse as a social problem

What allows one individual to feel a sense of entitlement and ownership over another? What is it about our society that not only allows, but perhaps even fosters these inequalities?

The statistics we have already seen tell us that domestic abuse occurs very frequently. If we wish to understand how it is that this can be happening, we need to have a long and truthful look at the society of which we are a part. Around us are countless ways in which some people are powerful while others are disempowered.

What social inequalities do you see around you each day? What disadvantages some people while others benefit? However much we strive towards social equality, these differences still exist: gender, socio-economic status, education, racial or cultural background, health and physical ability, age, or a host of other reasons. Our parish communities may include some people who have more status or power than others just because they belong to the right groups or social circles.

This can lead to some rather uncomfortable questions. Are there ways in which we benefit from these inequalities sometimes? Are there ways in which we foster them? Are there ways in which we fail to challenge them? If these inequalities are root causes of abuse, in a way, are we are all a part of the problem? Supporting an individual is one thing, but changing the hierarchical structure of society seems impossible.

Almost all of the rest of this book is a guide to helping on a much more individual level, but perhaps there are some things we can also do on a wider scale. We could:

- try recognising and challenging inequalities we see around us;

- think about how to educate our young people in equality, acceptance and healthy, respectful and consensual relationships, so that, as the next generation, they might do better than we have managed.

I certainly don't claim to have all the answers as to how to address the social level of the problem, but I do know that it is something that we need to be more aware of and more ready to acknowledge and discuss. We might not have the answers, but we can at least start asking the questions.

Endnotes

1 Women's Aid (www.womensaid.org.uk)
2 "Myths and Facts about Domestic Violence", Domestic Violence Intervention Program (www.dvipiowa.org)
3 Women's Aid SOS Save Refuges, Save Lives campaign (www.womensaid.org.uk)
4 Faith Trust Institute (www.faithtrustinstitute.org)

4

Understanding spiritual abuse

How is domestic abuse different for people in church communities?

You may presume that if you are experiencing domestic abuse but you are also a member of a church community, your experience probably won't be quite as bad. One would imagine that, surrounded by people who share the same beliefs, you would probably find it much easier to turn to other people for support, and that, inspired by their religious values, they would be ready to offer empathy and caring help.

The reality, unfortunately, is not quite so simple. While it can be true that people of faith can draw huge amounts of strength from their spiritual beliefs, there are also ways in which it can make dealing with domestic abuse more difficult. The examples below are from Christian church communities but the difficulties are the same for people from other faith communities as well.

It's dangerous to stay in the community if the perpetrator is still a part of it

When a victim/survivor leaves an abusive relationship, they may need to move to safe housing in a confidential location. It can be dangerous to keep in contact with anyone who might also be in contact with the perpetrator, particularly if they don't really understand how dangerous the perpetrator is. Many victim/survivors have to cut ties with the whole community in order to be safe.

Fear of losing their community might keep a victim trapped

When a victim/survivor has been isolated by abuse, their parish community is frequently their only social contact. Some will choose to stay with a perpetrator rather than risk losing their community. Some perpetrators will threaten to destroy the victim's relationship with their faith community in order to make them stay.

The perpetrator can use the community to abuse their partner

Perpetrators are often charming, manipulative and very good at getting sympathy from the people around them, and might use the community to further the abuse, for example by spreading false information about their victim.

The perpetrator might be a person of influence in the community

Perpetrators may have an important position within the parish. Where clergy are permitted to marry and have relationships, it is possible that the perpetrator may actually be the priest or religious leader.

Your parish community might be connected to your children's school

If your children go to a church school, it is likely that it is connected with your parish. Your children's school friends and their parents are probably involved in the same church and there can be a high risk of information getting to your abuser. In high-risk cases, the victim and children will need to move to a completely different area, which means the children will move schools. They might be unable to have much or any contact with old school friends if they are also involved in the same church community as the abuser.

The parish community might judge you for leaving your spouse

Strong family values are integral to most religious faiths and most of the time that is a positive thing. However, it can mean that some religious people find it harder to accept a choice to separate from a spouse or split up a family, even when that is actually the only safe option for the victim or children. Many victims have faced harsh judgement and criticism, or have even been ostracised by members of their church communities or by their church leaders.

Misinformed spiritual guidance is often dangerous

Research by the American organisation Faith Trust Institute[1] showed that victim/survivors of domestic abuse who have a religious faith are much more likely to turn to their faith leader than other professionals when they are seeking support.

Unfortunately, the majority are insufficiently trained to give informed and safe support. Many priests and faith leaders still approach domestic abuse from a reconciliation-focused approach. It cannot be stressed strongly enough that this approach is extremely dangerous and can even have fatal consequences.

The victim experiences spiritual abuse from their community and faith leaders as well as from the perpetrator

Someone commits spiritual abuse when they use religious or spiritual ideas to advise or pressurise a victim of domestic abuse to:

- stay with the perpetrator;

- forgive the perpetrator;

- believe the perpetrator's promises to change;

- rely on prayer rather than practical measures to keep safe;

- avoid support from domestic abuse organisations because they don't follow faith teachings;

- submit to their spouse.

What is spiritual abuse?

Spiritual abuse can take many forms, but in the context of domestic abuse there are three main kinds of spiritual abuse:

1. preventing someone from practising their religion or spirituality against their will;

2. forcing someone to practise a religion or spirituality against their will;

3. using a twisted form of religious or spiritual teaching in order to gain and maintain control over another person, or to coerce them to stay in an abusive relationship.

It is this last form of spiritual abuse that we will focus on here, because it has the highest capacity for damage.

In any of the major religions, there are passages which can be taken out of context and used for spiritual abuse. Here is an example from the Christian Bible, taken from Ephesians:

> Wives, be subject to your husbands as you are to the Lord. For the husband is the head of the wife just as Christ is the head of the church, the body of which he is the Saviour. Just as the church is subject to Christ, so also wives ought to be, in everything, to their husbands. [2]

Most of us, even those of us who are not experts in theology or Bible studies, are able to see these passages within the context of the wider Christian message of love, acceptance, equality and respect for others. What happens, though, if a male perpetrator wants to control and subjugate his wife? These words can become powerful tools of abuse. It doesn't even matter whether the perpetrator has any religious faith, only that the victim believes these words to be true.

If someone wants to control and manipulate another person, using a twisted form of their spiritual or religious beliefs can be the most powerful and devastating way of doing that. Yet spiritual abuse is still largely overlooked by most professionals working in the field of domestic abuse. This means that it is the responsibility of faith leaders and communities to work together with professionals and victim/survivors to end spiritual abuse.

Are we colluding with spiritual abuse?

No one wants to think of themselves as colluding with abuse of any kind, and certainly no one wants to think that their own spiritual or religious practice and belief could have the potential to harm another person. Yet collusion with spiritual abuse is much more common than you might imagine. Below is a list of "advice" given to real victim/survivors of domestic abuse:

- You made a promise: "in sickness and in health".

- You made a commitment to stay.

- Your husband is a good, religious man: he wouldn't do anything that bad.

- Go back and pray for God to heal your marriage.

- Prayer can heal everything. Leave it in God's hands.

- Pray to God to make you a better wife.

- Go and please your spouse – I will pray for you.

- Leaving your spouse is a sin – you will go to hell.

- You must accept this as part of God's plan for you.

- Offer up your suffering and give thanks for it, it makes you more holy.

- You must forgive whatever your abuser has done, no matter how many times he does it.

Every one of these statements is spiritual abuse, and yet every one of them was made by someone other than the perpetrator. Worse still, every one of them was made by someone to whom the victim had turned for help: a member of their faith community, a priest or a family member. These people have both enabled the perpetrator by colluding with abuse and themselves committed a dangerous form of abuse.

How common is spiritual abuse?

Unfortunately, horror stories reveal dreadful things said by representatives of the Church. A Spanish archbishop, for instance, claimed that domestic abuse is caused by women not obeying their husbands. He went on to say that women could avoid abuse if they didn't upset their husbands by asking for a separation or divorce.[3]

How many domestic abuse victims had turned to this priest, or others with similar views, to ask for help? Here in the UK, some priests have accused me of trying to destroy families by splitting up marriages. I have also met with countless victims damaged by spiritual abuse from their priest.

That is not to say that all priests or church representatives commit or collude with spiritual abuse. I have heard wonderful stories of people who have been given life-saving help from their priest or community. There are priests who actively campaign against abuse and offer incredible support to victims and survivors. But I also often hear very different stories: stories of terrible suffering, of lives endangered or destroyed, of communities ostracising victims or of priests sending people back into danger.

What does the Catholic Church actually have to say about domestic abuse?

Priests and other people who adopt a dangerous reconciliation-focused approach are actually not following the guidance of the Church. For example, the *Code of Canon Law* of the Catholic Church, the oldest continuously functioning legal system in the West, states:

> A spouse who occasions grave danger of soul or body to the other or to the children, or otherwise makes the common life unduly difficult, provides the other spouse with a reason to leave, either by a decree of the local Ordinary [for example, bishop] or, if there is danger in delay, even on his or her own authority.[4]

In other words, psychological, spiritual or physical abuse is sufficient reason to leave a spouse.

The Church of England has produced a policy and practical guide to responding well to domestic abuse. The document says that:

> domestic abuse in all its forms is contrary to the will of God and an affront to human dignity. All need to play their part in preventing or halting it.[5]

Other religions also teach that abuse is wrong. Nour, the organisation which supports Muslim victim/survivors of domestic abuse, says:

> Domestic abuse is a problem in Muslim communities. Ironically the teachings of this faith emphasise the rights of women and the rights of a wife in marriage. There are clear verses that speak out against oppressing one's spouse even during a divorce.[6]

Pope Francis has spoken several times about domestic abuse, making his position very clear. In his Episcopal exhortation *Amoris Laetitia* ("The Joy of Love") he recognised different forms of domestic abuse, including physical, sexual, psychological and financial abuse.

He then addressed what happens if someone needs to separate from their spouse because of abuse towards themselves or their children, saying that sometimes, separation is "morally necessary".

The Pope has talked about the Church's role in offering support to people who have experienced domestic or sexual abuse and the importance of training so that people can be sensitive to the needs of victim/survivors. It is equally important to teach young people about healthy and respectful relationships.

People who endanger victims by encouraging them to go back to abusive spouses are disregarding Church teaching. Most do not intend to commit spiritual abuse or to endanger lives, but their misguided actions can cause unimaginable harm. Christianity teaches that the sanctity of life is paramount. It is therefore of the highest importance to guide people in a way that protects the safety of those at risk of harm.
In the following chapters, we will look at some ways in which we can achieve that.

Endnotes

1 Faith Trust Institute (www.faithtrustinstitute.org)
2 Ephesians 5:22-24
3 http://www.stopabuseforeveryone.org/library/2-uncategorised/308-spain-archbishop-blames-domestic-violence-on-disobedient-wives.html
4 CIC 1153
5 You can download the whole document from https://www.churchofengland.org/sites/default/files/2017-11/responding-well-to-domestic-abuse-formatted-master-copy-030317.pdf
6 Nour (www.nour-dv.org.uk)

Mary's prayer

To the God who created me,

give me strength.

I need to find a way out,

to stop listening to those who take me away
from you.

Help me remember that you created me,

that you have great plans for me,

that there is light

and freedom

in you.

Mary,
a survivor of
domestic abuse

5

If you feel scared of your partner

This book is written for people wishing to learn how to support victim/survivors of domestic abuse. But I'm aware that there may be some of you reading this who have personal experience of abuse. You may have read the first few chapters of this book and recognised your own relationship in those pages.

Whether or not you feel the words "domestic abuse" apply to your situation, if you ever feel afraid of your partner, this chapter is for you. It is impossible in this short space to tell you everything I would like to, but here are seven things it might help you to know.

1. You are not alone

Cutting you off from other people is a common abusive tactic. Your partner does this to make you feel alone and powerless because that makes them feel more powerful. You might feel as though there is no one in the world who can really understand or help.

There are many women and men who are living with abuse right now, or who have been abused in the past. Some of them have shared their stories in this book to help you.

At the end of this book is a list of places you can contact to find people who understand and can help.

2. It's not your fault

- Abusers always blame their victims so that they avoid responsibility.

- Don't start believing that it is your fault.

- You are **never** responsible for your partner's abusive or aggressive behaviour. There is no excuse for abuse.

3. God does not want you to suffer

- God did not choose this for you.

- This is not part of your spiritual journey, intended to strengthen you.

- It is not a God-given punishment.

- You are not obliged to put up with it because you made a vow to someone you thought you could trust.

- You are being abused because someone has chosen to abuse you. It is not God's choice or your choice. It is your abuser's choice.

4. There is nothing wrong with you

Whatever it is that feels wrong, it isn't you. It's abuse that's wrong, not you.

5. There are people who understand and who can help

If you have already reached out for help and it didn't work for you, don't worry. That happens sometimes. Don't give up. The right help – organisations, groups, courses – is out there somewhere.

6. Safety comes first

If someone suggests something which feels dangerous, trust your instinct more than theirs. You know your situation better than they do.

7. You are important

Even if you feel worthless, that is just something that abuse makes you sometimes feel. You are important. You are precious and valuable. You deserve to be safe.

Michelle's prayer

Lord, protect me,
guide me,
keep me safe.
Grant me the strength, wisdom and good judgement
to know what to do in any situation.
Help me to know when and whom to ask for help.
Help me to value myself as you value me
and expect the love and respect you intend for me.
Help me to break old patterns that have harmed me
and put me at risk.
Help me to remember that I can say no to anything
that is not in my best interests.
Help me to remember that you made me to be in your image
as a precious child of God,
with my unique gifts and contributions to this wonderful world.
Help me to remove or avoid anything
that stands between me and my path,
my journey and all that makes me the best I can be.
Let me feel worthy of love,
and let your love in
to mend this broken heart, mind and life,
so I can be whole and wonderful.
In you I place my love and trust.
Protect me, Lord.
Amen.

Michelle, a survivor
of domestic abuse

6

How can I help someone else?

This chapter has more detailed information about ways in which you can help, but the following is a quick three-point summary of what you can do when someone is experiencing domestic abuse.

1. Is there urgent need for help?

Is it unsafe to go home?

If there is immediate danger, **call 999 straight away.** If the person needs an emergency injunction for their safety, contact the National Centre for Domestic Violence.[1]

2. Is there a child or vulnerable adult at risk of harm?

Is there immediate danger to the child?

If so **call 999 straight away.**

Are safeguarding measures needed?

If there is any risk of a child experiencing or witnessing violence, then safeguarding measures are needed.

- Follow the safeguarding procedure of your church or place of worship.

- If you are unsure what the procedure is, then contact your church's or diocesan safeguarding officer.

- If you are not a member of a church, or there is a reason you cannot contact the safeguarding officer, contact the NSPCC[2] or report directly to your local social services or your local domestic abuse organisation.

- **Always tell the victim/survivor that you are making a safeguarding report.** For their safety, it is vital that they are aware what is going on.

3. Is it a non-urgent situation?

Does the victim/survivor want specialist support?

- Inform the person about local, national or specialist support available.

- If it is unsafe for them to look up websites at home, or make calls from their own phone, offer them a safe place to do so.

- Do not give the person leaflets or books which would be dangerous to keep at home.

- If it is possible, offer to go with the person to their first appointment.

- Tell the person that you are still available if they want to talk to you again.

There is more information on page 79 about different kinds of support available.

Does the victim/survivor feel ready for specialist support?

- Never force or pressure someone to make contact with specialist support before they are ready, unless there is a safeguarding issue.

- Let the person know that:

  - you are there for them whenever they want to talk;

  - they have a right to support whenever or if ever they want it.

Safety awareness

Be aware that any intervention has the capacity to increase risk, so:

- always talk to the victim/survivor about everything you are doing;

- if it is not a safeguarding issue, don't act without the permission of the victim/survivor;

- always be guided by the victim/survivor's knowledge of their situation and of how they generally keep safe;

- be aware that perpetrators often check mobile phones or hack into email accounts of their victims, so always ask:

  - if it is safe to contact the victim/survivor;

  - what is the safest method of contact.

Knowing what different kinds of help are available

It often takes a whole team of professionals with different areas of expertise to deal with each situation of domestic abuse. There is also an important role for non-professional helpers. Make sure that a person feels that:

- they are not alone;

- you are there, not because it is your job, but because you want to be there for them.

This is not a comprehensive list, but here are some examples of the people who might offer specialist support:

- MARAC (Multi Agency Risk Assessment Conference) for high-risk cases;

- IDVAs (Independent Domestic Violence Advisors);

- helpline staff;

- refuge staff;

- Police Community Support Officers;

- DA Awareness course facilitators;

- social workers;

- Accident and Emergency staff;

- legal professionals;

- counsellors or psychotherapists;

- probation officers;

- perpetrator programme staff.

As a pastoral or lay helper, one of the most important things you can do is to signpost someone to specialist support.

Contacting the Police

If it is an emergency, always call 999 immediately.

If it is non-urgent, contact the police on 101.

The police have specially trained officers to deal with domestic abuse cases. They also work alongside other specialists who can provide support for housing, emotional or other needs.[3]

Contacting a domestic abuse agency

One way to work out the right kind of support is to contact a domestic abuse helpline or agency. They often have a range of different specialists, and can refer victim/survivors to the right one. There is a list of agencies at the end of this book.

What agencies offer can vary greatly from one area to another, so it's a good idea to have a sense of what is available in your area. Some organisations have specialist services for people with additional needs, such as providing linguistically and culturally accessible services for people from different backgrounds.

Contacting a counsellor or psychotherapist

Some agencies are only funded to work with people who are medium- and high-risk, so if someone is seen as a low-risk case, they won't qualify for support. If that is the case, the person might be happy just to have a friend to talk to, or they might want to see a counsellor or psychotherapist. Most counsellors and psychotherapists are not trained to work with domestic abuse, and don't realise that different skills and knowledge are needed. If you are contacting a counsellor or psychotherapist, make sure that they are properly trained and experienced to work with domestic abuse. **Couple or relationship therapy is not appropriate for domestic abuse** (see page 55).

Ruth's story

"Because my couple counsellor was unwilling or not trained to identify domestic abuse, she was taken in by my husband's charm, his position in society and his deference to her. She was also very scared of my husband's periodic anger – just enough to intimidate her. She responded by aligning herself with him, completely unwilling to talk about his abusive behaviour and only willing to discuss his dissatisfaction with the marriage. She became complicit in the ongoing abuse that happened between sessions.

She did not identify the abusive dynamic of the relationship and was unwilling to discuss the abusive behaviour I highlighted. After almost two years of therapy, it was my vicar, my GP and friends who intervened, identified my husband's abusive behaviour and helped me out of the marriage."

Where not to refer people for support

Certain kinds of support have been shown to be unhelpful for domestic abuse. Some may even do more harm than good. Below is a list of places **not** to refer people for help.

Don't suggest anger management training for the perpetrator

Perpetrators of domestic abuse can look very like people who are unable to control their temper. This has led many people to refer them to anger management courses for help.

- Abuse is not caused by an inability to control temper or aggression.

- Perpetrators use aggression to control their victim.

- Suggesting that the perpetrator has an anger management problem can enable them to avoid taking responsibility for the abuse: "I just lost control, I couldn't help myself."

Perpetrators need:

- specialist perpetrator programmes;

- to accept responsibility for their behaviour;

- to engage and make lasting changes.

It is potentially very dangerous for victim/ survivors to let out anger at their abuser, or hold in anger for years. Anger management techniques can help them to find safe ways to express their anger about their abuse.

Don't suggest relationship/couple therapy, family therapy or marriage enrichment programmes

Domestic abuse is **not** a marriage problem: it is an abuse problem. Suggesting relationship or family therapy can be very dangerous because:

- a victim of abuse cannot safely disclose abuse if the perpetrator is present;

- it is not possible to discuss safety strategies with the victim if the perpetrator is present;

- if a perpetrator witnesses their victim becoming more assertive or confident, it can make them feel less secure, increasing the risk of abusive behaviour becoming worse;

- perpetrators are often very skilled at manipulating professionals (including therapists) to collude with their abuse;

- relationship or family therapy often focuses on both partners taking equal responsibility for the couple's problems. In fact only the perpetrator is ever responsible for abuse, but they will usually project blame onto their victim. Relationship therapy can collude with victim-blaming and make the situation worse.

- it can be even more difficult for a victim who is working in relationship or family therapy to seek appropriate support;

- if a therapist recognises and challenges abuse in a way which makes the perpetrator feel exposed or vulnerable, the risk of escalation becomes much higher once the couple have returned home.

Is family therapy ever safe?

There are some very successful, well regarded and recommended programmes working with both the non-abusive parent and children helping them to overcome the effects of abuse. However it is only safe if the perpetrator is **not** involved.

What happens if a couple asks for relationship therapy but I think one partner is abusive?

If you are in any doubt as to whether relationship therapy is a safe option, it is better to be safe than sorry. The best way to handle the situation is to suggest that sometimes it's a good idea to work separately before working on a relationship together in therapy. **Remember that it isn't safe to talk about domestic abuse in front of the perpetrator!**

If you are making a referral, make sure that the individual therapists are trained to both recognise and work with domestic abuse.

At the time of writing, Caritas Westminster is piloting a programme called "Footsteps to Change" as a part of the Safe in Faith project. Footsteps to Change has specially trained practitioners who can work with perpetrators while a counsellor works with the victim/survivor.

Recognising the signs

Most victim/survivors don't tell you directly that they are being abused. They may disclose abuse indirectly, talking about "problems at home" or "marriage difficulties". Some might not disclose their abuse at all, so it is helpful to be able recognise the signs of abuse.

What are the signs?

Perpetrator:

- jealousy and possessiveness;
- control;
- imbalance of power in the relationship.

Victim/survivor:

- isolation;
- change in appearance or behaviour;
- self-neglect;

- fear of their partner or spouse;

- becoming reclusive;

- the person is never seen alone, only with their partner;

- their partner keeps checking where they are;

- no independent access to money;

- physical injuries.

Any one of these signs can mean that domestic abuse is happening. You will rarely see all of them at once. Often I have heard people say that they don't think abuse is happening because they haven't seen any signs of physical violence. It is really important to remember that:

- many kinds of serious abuse don't involve physical violence;

- perpetrators often inflict injuries where they are hidden from view.

Many victim/survivors will be very skilled at hiding the abuse for their own protection. It is not always helpful to rush in and talk directly about abuse. Some victim/survivors who are not ready to deal with their situation may get frightened off and feel less able to ask for help later on.

This doesn't mean that you stay silent; abuse thrives in silence. Just be careful about the language you choose. Abuse is a powerful word. It can be easier to start by talking about "difficult" or "controlling" relationships, or "scary" behaviour.

Endnotes

1 National Centre for Domestic Violence (www.ncdv.org.uk)
2 NSPCC (www.nspcc.org.uk/what-you-can-do/report-abuse/)
3 For more information about the police and domestic abuse, visit www.met.police.uk/advice-and-information/domestic-abuse/how-to-report-domestic-abuse/

7

Creating a safe helping environment

Opening up to someone about domestic abuse is scary and potentially dangerous.

- Never pressure someone to open up before they are ready, unless there is a safeguarding issue.

- Always create a safe environment which will make it more likely that someone will open up to you.

- Understand that the victim/survivor may be traumatised.

A safe physical environment where you can talk privately without being interrupted is important, but there are also qualities you can develop in yourself which help to build trust. Good support is always:

- non-judgemental;

- non-directive.

These qualities are vital because they are the opposite of an abusive relationship. Even if you think the person is making the wrong choice, it's important not to judge them or tell them what to do.

Reacting and responding

Later in this chapter, we are going to look at things we can do to respond safely to disclosures. Before that, it's important to be aware of some of the initial emotional reactions you might have. All of these reactions are natural and very common.

Unhelpful reactions to disclosures

- **Disbelief or minimisation** – this is especially common if you know the perpetrator.

- **Victim-blaming** – it's scary to think that domestic abuse could happen to any of us. It can be easier to believe that the victim must have done something to bring it on. But there is nothing a victim can do that would warrant or excuse abuse.

- **Feeling overwhelmed** – you can't fix everything yourself. That's what professional support is for.

- **Excessive anger** – this might make the victim/survivor feel that they need to defend the perpetrator and stand up for them against you!

- **Believing the perpetrator isn't that dangerous** – even if the perpetrator is someone you know, never underestimate how dangerous they can be.

- **Wanting to heal the relationship or save the marriage** – wanting to keep families together can be dangerous or even fatal when domestic abuse is happening.

Recognising any of these reactions in yourself doesn't mean that you are doing a bad job as a supporter. In fact, it is only by recognising these very natural reactions that we can rise above them. Only by being aware of our instinctive reactions can we actively choose our positive responses.

Safe responding to domestic abuse

When you are responding to a disclosure of domestic abuse, the three-point check at the beginning of Chapter 6 is a good place to start.

1. **Is it an emergency?** If so, **call 999 straight away.**

2. **Are children at risk?** If so, follow safeguarding procedures.

3. **Does the person want specialist help?** If so, give details of available help and find out if they need help to make contact safely.

It's important to be clear from the beginning about the kind of help you can and cannot offer. This will help avoid misunderstandings and help to build an open and trusting relationship between you.

Be clear about your limitations

Faced with someone who is scared or suffering, it can be tempting to promise you can make everything better. But to promise more than you can give and then let someone down could cause even more damage. Rather than trying to do too much yourself, it can be more helpful to give information about professional services and helplines.

Be clear about confidentiality

If a perpetrator finds out that their victim is seeking help, it can increase the risk of serious harm. In parish communities, it is easy for information to spread rapidly. Confidentiality can be life-saving – except where there is a safeguarding issue (for example if children or vulnerable adults are at risk). Then you are obliged to pass on that information to the relevant authorities.

If there are no safeguarding issues, but you still want to ask someone's advice about how to support a victim/survivor, ensure you give no information which could identify the person concerned. Remember that people are easily identified in small communities.

Be clear about safeguarding

All churches should have a safeguarding procedure. If you are working in a parish in any capacity, whether paid or voluntary, you should be aware of that policy. If you are concerned about the safety of a child or vulnerable adult, or if you want to know more about your safeguarding policy, contact your local parish safeguarding officer. If that isn't possible, for example if the safeguarding officer is closely connected to the situation or may even be the perpetrator, you should contact your diocese's safeguarding department.

If you are not working in a church or place of worship, or if none of the options above are available, then do one of the following:

- contact the NSPCC [1];

- contact your local domestic abuse agency for advice;

- contact your local social services to report the safeguarding issue.

What else can you do?

Give your time and understanding

If there is no urgent risk, and the individual does not want any other kind of help, just giving your time as a person to whom they can talk can make a huge difference.

Reassure them that abuse is wrong and it is not their fault

There is no excuse for abuse. But when someone has been living with abuse, abusive thoughts can start to feel true. It is important to reassure all victim/survivors that none of the abuse is their fault.

Encourage them to create a safety plan

This is a plan of what they will do if things get dangerous at home. A safety plan might involve things like:

- carrying keys, money and your phone with you all the time;

- making arrangements for where you would go if it's dangerous to stay;

- keeping passports and important documents somewhere safe.

Each safety plan is unique and it is important that the victim/survivor chooses what goes into theirs.[2]

Help the person access support safely

Perpetrators of domestic abuse often check their victim's phones, emails or browsing history. They may also demand to know where their victim is at every moment of the day and some ask to see evidence. Providing a victim/survivor with a safe place to use the phone or internet can create an opportunity to access support. Offering to accompany them to appointments might give the confidence they need to move towards safety.

Before giving leaflets or books always check it is safe to take them home; you may need to arrange a safe place to leave them instead. Domestic abuse support websites have information about how to cover your tracks if the perpetrator has access to the computer.

Make a record of what you hear

If the person gives you permission, make notes as soon as possible about what they have told you. Always keep these notes safely and confidentially.

Check up on them – safely

It is never safe to check up on someone in a way that the perpetrator might find out about. However, if the victim/survivor wants it, arrange safe ways of regularly checking on their safety.

Work alongside the specialist services

This is more appropriate for people helping in the capacity of pastoral carer, although sometimes friends or relatives can keep in contact with specialist support.

Each church community could have a designated person who contacts their local domestic abuse services to introduce themselves and make a connection. This can make referring individuals much easier and also makes it easier to share relevant and appropriate information.

Make sure that the person feels valued and believed

When someone has been experiencing domestic abuse, however strong they are, their confidence will be affected. The difference you can make by giving your time, listening, believing and making someone feel valued and important is difficult to express.

Endnotes

1   NSPCC (www.nspcc.org.uk/what-you-can-do/report-abuse/)
2   You can find out more information about making a safety plan at www.womensaid.org.uk/the-survivors-handbook/making-a-safety-plan/

8

Giving spiritual support

Nora's story

"We used to go to a monthly prayer group. The people in our group meant a lot to me: I didn't have many other friends. My husband was very charming and popular. They had no idea what he was really like. At home he was a very scary man. When I finally left him and took the children, he went to our friends in the prayer group and told them he didn't know why I had left him and he was distraught. They gave him loads of sympathy. I called up one of them and they told me I shouldn't come to the prayer meetings any more. I could just imagine them judging me for destroying a family and I felt the pressure to go back. I felt so alone: it was one of my worst moments. When I tried to talk to people whom I thought were my friends, they just told me to talk to my counsellor. It felt like the only reason someone would listen to me was if I paid them. It made me feel so worthless."

If you are supporting someone through your church, one of the most important things you can provide is spiritual support. It is extremely rare for specialist professionals to address religion or spiritual abuse. A religious person's faith is central to the way in which they understand everything, including their abuse. For people of faith, it can be difficult for any other kind of help to be effective unless they also have the opportunity to explore their abuse from a spiritual perspective.

Below are some of the important things you need to know about providing spiritual support for victim/survivors of domestic abuse.

Understand how spiritual abuse is used by perpetrators of domestic abuse

Perpetrators of domestic abuse:

- will seek out passages from the Bible or from their victim's own sacred texts which, taken out of context, will appear to support their right to abuse;

- do not need to believe the passages;

- do not need to share the same faith background;

- will use these passages in order to gain and maintain power and control over their victims;

- will often make use of commonly-held ideas about religious beliefs and marriage (even if totally untrue) in order to control or trap their victim. An example of this is perpetrators (and others) telling victims that, for Catholics, divorce is a mortal sin. It is not. But many Catholic victims have felt trapped in dangerous marriages because they believed it was.

Spiritual abuse can also be carried out by other members of the victim/survivor's family or faith community, who will repeat these twisted messages. The victim/survivor will start to believe things such as:

- This abuse is part of God's plan for me.

- God is punishing me for some wrong I have done in the past.

- Suffering makes people more holy.

- I have to accept whatever abuse I experience and turn the other cheek.

- I am a bad person if I don't forgive everything my abuser does to me.

- I should do whatever my husband says – when I don't, he has the right to abuse me.

- It would be sinful to think about leaving.

Be familiar with the teachings of your faith about gender equality, healthy relationships and abuse

While it is helpful to be able to challenge the twisted messages of spiritual abuse, victim/survivors frequently need more than this in order to really free themselves from its effects. It is also important to be familiar with the official guidance for people dealing with domestic abuse. We have seen how easily information becomes corrupted. It is well worth encouraging people from any faith background to check what the actual guidance of their faith is on the matter of domestic abuse. Listed at the end of this book are helping organisations who work with different faith groups.

Understand how to challenge internalised spiritual abuse

When someone lives with abuse for a long time it becomes internalised. Abusive thoughts start to feel like the victim's own thoughts. Most therapists working with victim/survivors will address internalised abuse, but very few address internalised spiritual abuse.

When abuse is spiritual, the internalised abuse is even more powerful because it really feels like the victim's spiritual or religious teachings. It can even feel like the voice of God. How can we challenge that? A starting point can be asking the victim/survivor questions like these:

- What do you think God is like?

- How do you think God feels about you?

- How does God want you to feel?

- What do you think a loving God thinks about the things that have been happening to you?

These questions can help a victim/survivor:

- to get back in touch with the feeling of God's love;
- to recognise and challenge thoughts coming from internalised spiritual abuse;
- to discover a tool they can use by themselves whenever the need arises.

These kinds of questions are usually much more effective than theological discussion.

Some people have been so damaged by abuse that they can't even imagine God's love for them because they feel so unworthy of love. For these people, your role is even more important; you can be a mirror of that love in the love and respect that you show to the victim/survivor through your words and actions.

Be aware that when you are dealing with a child who has been abused by a parent, or an adult abused in childhood, the language of God as Father or Mary as Mother can create difficulties. In these cases it is better to avoid the parent imagery and focus on the idea of God as Love.

Spiritual abuse and forgiveness

Many perpetrators use the idea of forgiveness to spiritually abuse their victim: "You have to forgive me every time, it says so in the Bible." Some survivors do choose to forgive their perpetrator, but it is important that:

- forgiveness is their choice;
- they are first safe from further abuse.

Pressuring someone to forgive their abuser before they are ready is not only potentially dangerous: it is a form of spiritual abuse.

Domestic abuse and annulments

Some people who have separated from an abusive spouse may consider having the marriage annulled. Recent changes have made the application process simpler.

The people working in the tribunals:

- are very familiar with dealing with situations of domestic abuse;

- will advise and assist with annulment processes;

- will never contact a former spouse without your permission;

- will not reveal your current address.

Creating abuse-free communities

As well as supporting individual victim/survivors of domestic abuse, it is important to look to the future and work together to create domestic-abuse-free communities. This may feel like an impossible task, but there are things we can all do to raise awareness of abuse in your community:

- Recognise and challenge any ideas which may result in the oppression of individuals or groups.

- Openly work towards a community where everyone is valued and treated equally.

- Encourage all community members to do the same.

- Educate young people about healthy, safe, respectful relationships.

- Give sermons on:

  - healthy relationships and gender equality;

  - abuse and broken relationships.

- Let victim/survivors know that your church is a safe place to come and ask for help. It will also make it much harder for perpetrators to use religion to justify their behaviour.

- Lead by example with gender equality and respect. This is particularly important where the priesthood is exclusively male.

9

Working with perpetrators

Working with perpetrators is challenging, and full of risks. Many perpetrators are highly skilled at manipulating people into colluding with abuse, even people who are trying to help the victim/survivor.

Below are two important tips for dealing with perpetrators.

1. NEVER approach a perpetrator

As a lay helper, it is **never** appropriate for you to approach a perpetrator to talk about the abuse even if you know the person quite well. It lets them know that:

- the victim/survivor has told someone about the abuse;

- the victim/survivor is asking for help.

Either of these is likely to put the victim/survivor at risk. The perpetrator may well react to you in a way that seems appropriate, even remorseful, but it is usually a very different story once they are at home with their victim.

2. What to do if a perpetrator approaches you to ask for help

If a perpetrator asks for help to change their abusive behaviour, the best thing to do is recommend a perpetrator programme. Always wait for the perpetrator to request help before suggesting this.

A perpetrator is more likely to approach you as part of a couple who are "facing marriage difficulties". You may either suspect or know that one of the partners is abusing the other. When this happens, **don't try to work with a couple together**. Couple therapy, marriage enrichment programmes, mediation or family therapy are not recommended for domestic abuse.

A much more helpful intervention would be to recommend specialist therapy for the victim/survivor and a specialist programme for the perpetrator.[1] However, it is essential to make these recommendations with extreme care. Unless the word "abuse" has been used by the couple, it could be very dangerous for you to use that language. It is usually helpful to use the language that is used by the couple themselves; for example, if they talk about behaviour which is "frightening" or "controlling", then suggest specialist help to deal with that.

In some cases, particularly if you suspect abuse, the only safe option is to suggest speaking to each partner individually, and then to suggest support for the victim/survivor in confidence, without the knowledge of the perpetrator.

Some rules for staying safe around perpetrators

- Don't assume that their acknowledgement of their abuse makes them less dangerous.

- Don't try to help them yourself unless you know what you are doing.

- Don't be taken in by apparent repentance or conversions.

- Don't be taken in by "reasons" for abusive behaviour like addiction, health issues or previously being a victim.

- Do not excuse or minimise any of their behaviour.

- Do not collude with religious or spiritual abuse.

- Check on the wellbeing of the victim/survivor.

- Make sure that the victim/survivor has access to appropriate support.

- If children or vulnerable adults are at risk you must follow safeguarding procedures.

- Do not try to offer support yourself.

- Do tell the perpetrator that the abuse needs to stop and recommend professional help.

- Do not refer the person to anger management specialists or to general counsellors or psychotherapists. Only refer the person to a professional or organisation trained to work with perpetrators.

- Only refer the perpetrator to a service that engages with the victim and checks that they are safe through the process.

- Don't encourage reconciliation just because the perpetrator is asking for help to change.

- Don't think that the perpetrator is no longer dangerous just because they are asking for help to change.

- Always be mindful of your own safety. Perpetrators can be dangerous people.

- Never meet with a perpetrator in a private place.

- Do not agree to advocate for the perpetrator or provide a character witness for them.

Endnotes

1 You can find more information about perpetrators and where to get help from www.respect.uk.net

10

Self-care and safety for helpers

When you are faced with someone in such distress it's easy to forget about your own needs, or to feel guilty for looking after yourself. Working with these kinds of issues, it is easy to feel overwhelmed by someone else's needs, or to become drained if we are not careful.

Below are a few self-care tips:

- Be aware of your own safety. Never visit a victim/survivor's home if the perpetrator might be there. Make sure that you meet victim/survivors in a safe place.

- Be aware that perpetrators can be extremely dangerous. Never approach the perpetrator even if you think you know them.

- Understand that you can't fix this by yourself. Make use of other professionals or organisations offering help.

- Make sure that you have access to the information you need. This can be through a local organisation or helpline, or through line management if you are working as a volunteer or helper in your place of worship.

- If you are working as a volunteer, make sure you have adequate training and support.

- Be clear about your boundaries from the start. Promising more than you can deliver is damaging for you and for the person you are helping.

- Take good care of yourself physically; eat well, sleep well and exercise.

- Find things that help you to switch off and create regular "down time" doing things you enjoy.

- Have someone you trust to whom you can talk to when things feel difficult. Be careful not to breach confidentiality when you are offloading.

- Listen to your own emotions.

- Be aware of how your own resilience varies depending on what is going on in your life. If you are dealing with difficulties yourself, you will have less strength available for supporting others.

- If you have been through something similar yourself, be aware how supporting someone else might affect you: it could bring back some traumatic memories. Make sure that you have access to proper support yourself.

Victim/survivors of domestic abuse are among the bravest and most inspiring people I have known. The opportunity to share their journey has been one of my life's great privileges. I hope that this book has inspired you to learn more, to become more aware of those suffering, often in silence, around you and to offer yourselves as a beacon of light in the darkness.

Philippa's prayer

Lord, thank you,
I love you.
You saw me before I saw myself.

Lord, thank you,
I am amazed by you.
You believed in me when I lost hope in myself.

Lord, thank you,
I love you.
You guided me, I listened and today I am free.

Philippa, a survivor
of domestic abuse

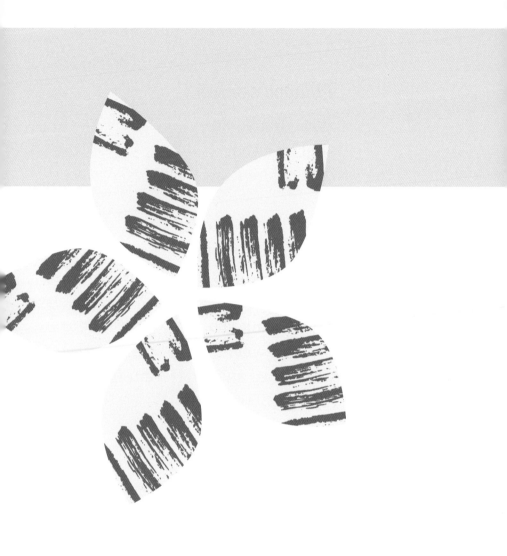

Organisations and resources
For support in faith communities

CEDAR (Catholics Experiencing Domestic Abuse Resources):
www.cedar.uk.net
A range of resources to help parishes, deaneries, dioceses, schools and organisations in the Catholic Church in England and Wales grow in awareness of the issues surrounding domestic abuse.

Jewish Women's Aid: www.jwa.org.uk
Free helpline: 0800 801 0500

The only specialist organisation in the UK supporting Jewish women affected by domestic violence and abuse.

Kahrmel Wellness: www.kahrmelwellness.com:
An interfaith organisation dedicated to assisting adult and child survivors of DVA to rebuild and restore their lives.

Nour: www.nour-dv.org.uk
A charity which aims to engage the public, and especially the minority Muslim communities, to become aware of and take action against domestic violence.

Restored: www.restoredrelationships.org
An international Christian alliance to transform relationships and end violence against women. It aims to answer two questions: "Where is the Church?" and "Where are the men?" when it comes to ending violence against women. Email info@restoredrelationships.org for more information or to join this community.

Safe in Faith: www.caritaswestminster.org.uk
A project being developed by Caritas Westminster to provide access to support for domestic and spiritual abuse.

Safety Across Faiths and Ethnic (SAFE) Communities Project (Standing Together)

Empowering communities to respond to domestic abuse. Providing training in faith communities. Email h.jawad@standingtogether.org.uk or call 0208 748 5717 for more information about accessing the project.

For general domestic abuse support

24-hour National Domestic Violence Helpline

Tel: 0808 2000 247
www.nationaldomesticviolencehelpline.org.uk/
Run in partnership between Women's Aid and Refuge (see below).

AAFDA (Advocacy After Fatal Domestic Abuse): www.aafda.org.uk
Helping families get victims' voices heard.

DeafHope UK (SignHealth): www.signhealth.org.uk
Support for Deaf women experiencing domestic abuse.

National Centre for Domestic Violence: www.ncdv.org.uk
A fast emergency injunction service.

National LGTB+ Domestic Abuse Helpline

Tel: 0800 999 5428
Email: help@galop.org.uk

NSPCC: www.nspcc.org.uk
The UK's leading children's charity.

Refuge: www.refuge.org.uk
Providing a range of life-changing and life-saving services.

RESPECT: www.respect.uk.net
Support for men experiencing domestic abuse and information about perpetrator programmes.

Respond: www.respond.org.uk
Specialist help for people with learning disabilities.

The Freedom Programme: www.freedomprogramme.co.uk
Domestic violence programme designed for women victims.

The Hideout: www.thehideout.org.uk
Website to help children and young people understand domestic abuse.

Women's Aid: www.womensaid.org.uk
A grassroots federation working together to provide life-saving services and build a future where domestic violence is not tolerated.

Add your local services here:

Further Reading

Lundy Bancroft, *Why Does He Do That? Inside the minds of angry and controlling men* (New York: Berkley Publishing, 2002).

Lundy Bancroft and Jac Patrissi, *Should I Stay or Should I Go? A guide to knowing if your relationship can – and should – be saved* (New York: Berkley Publishing, 2011).

Pat Craven, *Living with the Dominator* (London: Freedom Publishing, 2008), also available as a free download.

Pat Craven, *Freedom's Flowers: the effects of domestic abuse on children* (London: Freedom Publishing, 2012).

Connie Fourré, *Finding Your Way Through Domestic Abuse – a guide to physical, emotional and spiritual healing* (Notre Dame, IN: Ave Maria Press, 2006).

Patricia Evans, *Controlling People – how to recognise, understand and deal with the people who control you* (Avon, MA: Adams Media, 2003).

Sandra Horley, *Power and Control: Why Charming Men Can Make Dangerous Lovers* (London: Vermillion, 2002).

Rosalind B. Penfold, *Dragonslippers: this is what an abusive relationship looks like* (London: Harper Press, 2006).